THE BEAR

by Maria Valasquez

Printed in the United States of America

ISBN 0-15-314549-8

Ordering Options
ISBN 0-15-314559-5 (Grade K Collection)
ISBN 0-15-314562-5 (package of 5)

Harcourt Brace School Publishers

3 4 5 6 7 8 9 10 179 2002 2001

the bear

the bird

the pig

3

the monkey

the seal

the mouse

the puppy

the bear

TAKE-HOME BOOK
Use with "Jesse Bear, What Will You Wear?"